# The Mysteries

## a verse play

## William Considine

SPUYTEN DUYVIL
*New York City*

## Acknowledgements

Thank you to:

Rose-Marie Brandwein, John Payne, Allan Brown, Elizabeth Caruso, Eric Diamond, Meliora Dockery, Albert Insinnia, Emil G. Keller, Cam Kornman, and Carla Torgrimson (Polaris North) Chris Brandt, Sara Costantino, Mark Gering, Richard Keyser, April Leonhard, Cameron McIntosh, Ward Nixon, Eve Packer, and Barbara Vann (Medicine Show Theatre), Elae Moss Benedetto (Exit Strata), Kevin O'Brien, George Alvers, Roger Best, Anders Bolang, Steven Booker, James Loutzenhiser, Suzanne Turner, Bob Holman, and Elinor Nauen (St. Marks Poetry Project Poets Theater Festival at La Mama), Kristina Marie Darling

ISBN 978-1-963908-60-2

Cover art by Deborah Gans

Library of Congress Control Number: 2025944751

For Rose-Marie Brandwein and the players of Polaris North

# Synopsis

*The Mysteries* is set in archaic Greece, at the birth of Western civilization. It is based on a story in Plutarch's *Life of Solon*.

In archaic Athens, talk of war is forbidden, under penalty of death, after a long war with the neighboring city, Megara. The Athenian women's mystery festival of goddess worship at Eleusis is being restored, after cessation during the long war. But Athens is still tense with poverty, enslavement for unpaid debt, and civil unrest.

Solon, a poet and sea trader, is inspired by the Oracle at Delphi to seek political power. Pretending to be insane to avoid the death penalty, he recites a poem in the marketplace to urge war again. He claims Megarians plan to kidnap women at the women's mysteries. He is made leader of an armed group sent to defend the women.

Solon sends his young cousin, Pisistratus, to lure a few Megarians to the women's mysteries. Solon and his armed group disrupt the women's ritual. Disguising themselves as women, they kill the Megarians when they arrive. The women leave their mystery festival unfinished, after the desecration.

The young goddess Persephone emerges from the ritual site to promise Solon that all his efforts will lead to endless war and new forms of enslavement.

# Characters

Prologue Speakers    a modern woman and a woman of ancient Greece, any age

Solon          a poet of Athens, male 40

Pisastratus    his cousin, male 20

Cleinias       a ship owner, male 45

Farmer One    male, any age

Farmer Two    male, any age

Ion    Temple Keeper of the Delphic Oracle, male

Python    a priestess, the Oracle of Apollo at Delphi, female 25

A bound man and two guards    males

Myrto    Solon's wife, female 35

Archon    chief magistrate of Athens, a one-year term, male 50

Basilinna    a noblewoman, female 50

Hierophant    priestess of the earth goddesses at Eleusis, female 50

Euturpe    a dissenting woman, female 40

Persephone    girl goddess, Queen of the Dead, female 25


Two armed men with a woman and man bound for enslavement.

Two armed men with a different man bound for enslavement.

Chorus of Women of Athens, female, any age

Wrestlers, crowd, soldiers in battle array, soldiers dressed as women, Megarian men

Possible doubling of parts:

Python—Persephone—Chorus - Euturpe

Cleinias or a Farmer - Temple Keeper - Soldier

Prologue Speakers—Chorus—Basilinna—Heirophant—Euturpe

Farmers One and Two—Crowds—Soldiers - Megarians

Archon - Soldier

Armed slavers and their captives—soldiers, Megarians


Note: in a staged reading, ten actors served with doubling of parts.

# Settings

*Prologue:* the stage

1 *Wrestlers:* an outdoor area in Athens, ca. 600 B.C.

2 *Oracle:* the temple of Apollo at Delphi

3 *A New Slave:* a path on the outskirts of Athens

4 *Home:* the home of Solon and Myrto

5 *Procession:* the Stoa and marketplace of Athens

6 *A Mad Poet:* the Stoa and marketplace of Athens, next morning

7 *The Rites:* the shrine of the earth goddesses at Eleusis

8 *The Goddess:* the Cavern of Hell


Note that the time is prior to the classical period.
It's a poor, simple world.
The Eleusinian Mysteries are conflated in this work
with the secret women's festival rites of Athens,
about which even less is known, for dramatic purposes.

# Prologue

*The PROLOGUE SPEAKERS, who are a MODERN WOMAN in contemporary clothes and a WOMAN OF ANCIENT GREECE, enter.*

MODERN WOMAN
Ancient Greece is the scene, early
Greece, centuries before the Classic Age,
emerging from myth into glimpses of
memory, a golden fleece and then this:
olive groves on hills, sheep roaming
mountains like clouds. Athens, source
of the Western world, is a crowded town.
Above is a rock fortress, the Acropolis.
These people rode the bright sea.
They caught wind in one sail
or rowed together in a rhythm of whole bodies.
They clung to coastlines and harbors, then
darted over wide sea to Egypt, Libya, Sicily.
But an ordinary rainstorm passing
like a veil across the sea
onto men in open boats was terror,
sometimes shipwreck and drowning.
Our tale tonight is a few facts
emerging out of mythic thinking.
So many people have tried to penetrate
the misted, dreamy sources of memory.
The darkest parts will always be hidden.

GREEK WOMAN
Athena! Goddess with a shield, sheltering
life in cities! We've seen too much war!
Long, sporadic, harassing campaigns, raids,
pirates scrambling from their boats ashore,
rushing shouting death into workaday cities,
burnt crops, burnt homes, murder,
war between neighboring towns—cousins clash,
bleed and die in the curse of iron and bronze.

MODERN WOMAN
Megara and now-famous Athens are towns
close by one another, on the same coast.
Between them is Eleusis, the shrine
of the earth goddess, the core of the world.
They fight for many years over lands
between them and an island just offshore,
to feed their bustling towns.

GREEK WOMAN
Weary, drained of tears and blood of long years
of war, we've negotiated peace.

MODERN WOMAN
Athens gets the shrine at Eleusis
with farms and pastures round.
Megara gets the island of Salamis,
in the bay the cities don't exactly share.

GREEK WOMAN
We can go to earth's mother goddess
again at Eleusis! There Demeter wept
at a well, for death, till she saw rebirth.
It's the cave entrance to death's domain.
We can revive the rites of worship there,
secret rites: women's Mysteries!

MODERN WOMAN
To keep peace, both cities enact a law
strange to our ears: it's forbidden to talk
of war, propose war, demand war.

GREEK WOMAN
The punishment for war talk is death!

MODERN WOMAN
This moment of peace is the start of the story.

*MODERN WOMAN exits.*
*ANCIENT GREEK WOMAN remains onstage.*

# Scene One: Wrestlers

*Scene: an outdoor area in Athens, ca. 600 B.C.E.*
*The ANCIENT GREEK WOMAN from the prologue is onstage.*
*SEVERAL MEN enter from different directions and begin stretching*
*and exercising.*
*They include PISASTRATUS, CLEINIAS, FARMER ONE, FARMER TWO.*
*Some practice together with spear and shield.*

GREEK WOMAN
An elder of my tribe told me: at the next moon,
the women of Athens will all leave the city.
We'll go in procession to the shrine
of the earth goddess. And we'll perform again
the mysteries of the double goddess.
Beauty is reborn: we'll go in peace.

FARMER ONE
And when can we work the new fields there?

GREEK WOMAN:
This ritual comes first in tradition.

FARMER ONE
We're too close to hunger to wait longer.

GREEK WOMAN
War planted torn bodies and burned off
the ripening grains we needed. Now we can
give proper respect to the earth goddess.
We'll prosper again in peace.

FARMER ONE

I can't wait.

FARMER TWO

The great families of the city will take
possession, and their debt slaves will till
the new lands. If you want to plant those fields,
then let your debts continue unpaid.
Soon we'll see you bending over
to seed the new land under the lash.

GREEK WOMAN

Please don't joke about debt slaves.
My tribeswoman just lost two children
to the slavers. She and her husband are frantic
with grief and shame. The crop yield was not
enough to pay their debt for rent, seeds and food.

FARMER ONE

It's shameful. Will they be sold abroad?

GREEK WOMAN

Or to the silver mines? Which is worse?

FARMER ONE

I fought Megarians for the new land.
I'd go there tomorrow with a plow and ox—
if I could borrow a plow and ox.

FARMER TWO
Pledging yourself for debt repayment?

FARMER ONE
This women's ritual is a show
to give time to the great and rich
for their claims to grow out of the ground
– that what our armies won is theirs.

PISASTRATUS
Watch what worry makes you say. Some thoughts
that may be plain to you are forbidden.

FARMER ONE
What is forbidden is talk of war.
I'm talking about farming for my family.

PISASTRATUS
You make your living sound like civil war.

CLEINIAS
The first families have a good claim too.
They financed the wars with armor and rations
and brought horses to battle. They led.
Till ownership is settled, the land will
be leased to the highest bidders. Their slaves
will work it, or sharecroppers.

*TWO ARMED MEN enter, accompanying a BOUND WOMAN and BOUND MAN.*
*They cross the stage.*

FARMER ONE
Let them go! How could you do this?

FARMER TWO
Keep them together! Don't separate families!

GREEK WOMAN
Do you have children?

BOUND WOMAN
They were taken last year.

GREEK WOMAN
Where were they sold?

BOUND WOMAN
I don't know! Onto a ship!

*The ARMED MEN exit with the BOUND WOMAN and BOUND MAN.*
*GREEK WOMAN goes with them.*

CLEINIAS
It's a terrible sight—but what we need
to see is payment of his debt.
And someone has to work the mines.
It's a great source of our wealth!

FARMER ONE
Their children already taken...

CLEINIAS

Awful, yes, but pledging yourself first
won't help your children when you're taken.
And children are good for the mines.
They work in smaller spaces.
It saves so much digging.

FARMER ONE

They're children!

CLEINIAS

They're less strong and tire easily, yes.
Not ideal. But they're fed. They live on.

FARMER ONE

It's a dreadful life and early death.

PISASTRATUS

Keep your spirit fired up. You'll find friends.
Many feel as you do, friend, but not yet
so loud and outright demanding.

FARMER ONE

I do demand!

FARMER TWO

Come wrestle, then, fighter.

FARMER ONE and FARMER TWO wrestle. The OTHERS exercise.
SOLON enters.

PISASTRATUS
Solon! Please tell us again
your poem of the dolphins.

SOLON
No one came to the playing field
to hear me sing about dolphins.

PISASTRATUS
Wherever there's an audience, poet!
There's a lot of heat rising over the land.
Give us some sea spray to cool us off.

CLEINIAS
Yes! A poem! And a flute girl! And wine!

SOLON
Well, they'll all be suggested in:
"The Dolphin."
The sea intoxicates me.
When I look inside its bright waters,
I see my head darken
and float like I do on wine,
drifting far away and back.
Thoughts play ahead
like dolphins leading my ship.
Sleek, leaping families
of dolphins sing in bubbles
as soft as the foam on the lip
of wine you just poured.
The sun on the swaying sea
licks the earth's liquid exultation.

CLEINIAS

Thank you! It sounds like your heart's still at sea.

SOLON

I'd like to ride the sea back to Egypt
again, yes.

CLEINIAS

These will be good times for trade.
Peace will mean safe passage. A young man can
get rich now, lugging jugs of oil up the Nile.

SOLON

I only trade to travel and see more.

CLEINIAS

And you've restored your family's fortunes!

SOLON

You know the basics: the painted jar's
worth as much as the oil inside it.
Can you rent me three ships and crews,
for two months this summer?

CLEINIAS

We'll talk. Come join me for dinner
next week, before the women leave.


*CLEINIAS exits.*

SOLON
He'll deal. Come with me to Egypt.

PISASTRATUS
It's a long voyage.

SOLON
Cousin, it's another world.

PISASTRATUS
Thank you, but
I'm not a boy anymore, and not
a voyager. I have my own plans in mind.
It's not right to press me anymore.
I'll throw you down.

SOLON
Yes, let's wrestle.

*SOLON and PISASTRATUS oil themselves.*

PISASTRATUS
Why leave the city when so much is at stake?
The war's over, but now all's changeable
and tense. It's time for new men to step up.

SOLON
Like everyone, I'm exhausted, from years
of recurring battle with Megarians.
I want to work for myself and build wealth.

PISASTRATUS

Peace seems fit for tradesmen and women,
but the nobles watch, restless for war.
We're of noble birth.
And discontent is festering, the debts
pit all against all within the city.

SOLON

You listen too much to what's unsaid.
The punishment for war talk is death,
and there's sense in that. Words beat drums
and pulses pound too fast, too giddy, feeling
blood flow. Let your heart race over
the sea, to easy, exotic pleasures.

PISASTRATUS

You'd rather talk about money and wine.

SOLON

I would, yes.

PISASTRATUS

Old stories and young women.

SOLON

Yes! Good!

PISASTRATUS

You're just a sweet talker—a poet.

SOLON
I can still pin you squirming.


FARMER ONE and FARMER TWO *cease wrestling and step to the rear.*
*SOLON and PISASTRUS wrestle.*
*PISASTRATUS throws SOLON.*


SOLON
Let's go slow.
I want to write a poem, yes, one
that will last for ages. Priests far up the Nile
have told me things Greeks lost in the Flood.
Great storms stripped good soil and homes off
our Acropolis, leaving that rough, high rock.
Egypt saw all and remembered.
They baked the past into clay signs.
Men who can read the walls of tombs
told me such a story, an ancient city
in the sea, called Atlantis.

PISASTRATUS
The city shining on the sea like the sun.

SOLON
You've heard of it?

PISASTRATOS
You told me about it.

SOLON

You see, I need to tell that story.
It's an epic tale, giving shape to the past.
It's the best since Homer sang and
gave the cup to glory, toasting war.
Come with me to Egypt with jugs of
olive oil. We'll learn more of their stories.
We'll earn gold, enough to squander years.
I'll spend those years on one poem—Atlantis.


PISASTRATUS

You like to gawk at barbarians,
marvel at their tales and eat bizarre food.
I don't like to leave my city.
Leadership is my own strange dream,
my epic path to manhood's glory.


SOLON

You'll need gold.


PISASTRATUS and SOLON wrestle again.
PISASTRATUS throws SOLON.


PISASTRATUS

You should splash alone with your dolphins.
You can rave about lost cities and tombs,
but the young men of Athens want to hear
more about what is forbidden.


SOLON

What little is forbidden is not worth discussing.

PISASTRATUS

What is forbidden is to speak
while the island Salamis lies on her back
in the bay and Megarians play upon her,
looking over and laughing at Athens.

SOLON

No one cares more for Salamis than me.
But there's more on the earth than that one island.
Open your eyes to a wider world..

PISASTRATUS

Stop your idle dreaming. Look and listen
to what young men say as we sit idle
—or what we now are stopped from saying.
Can you say in a poem what can't be said?

SOLON

That's what we'll learn in the oldest cities
of Egypt, where it's written on the walls.
Their scribes love to hear our Greek verses.
Our lively meter dances in daylight,
beyond the vast shadows of their tombs.
They'll pay us well. We'll skip the middlemen.
The journey overseas and far up the Nile,
into kingdoms of the dead, to long-buried
riches, is for brave men. It's glory. It's for you.

PISASTRATUS

Too many graves and strange gods, and stranger food.

*THEY wrestle. SOLON throws PISASTRATUS.*

SOLON

Don't come with me, then. Forget it. Still,
get beyond this little city seething with
resentments and debts. Go colonize
on the Black Sea coast, that's a great exploit.
Hire poets to sing of your glory.

PISASTRATUS

Colonizing, even trade, is dangerous,
while Megara rules our harbor. I'll stay,
wrestling, training, planning for the city.
Politics and war is a man's life.

SOLON

I was hoping to interest you in more.
I guided you to manhood. Cousin,
I love in you the fire, the boldness
that could someday lead Athens.
But put that passion into peaceful play.
Don't rush to spill your hot blood.

PISASTRATUS

The youth of Athens were raised as warriors.
Now we're to be playful sheep. My fire?
It burns me. I'm a roasting lamb. The cliques
of leading families will feast in peace.

*THEY wrestle again. PISASTRATUS pins SOLON.*

Who can say what is forbidden?
Who can say what can't be said?
He will lead the youth of Athens.
That's more urgent work for a poet
than tales of sunken cities and dolphins.
Don't woo me anymore with talk of trade
and travel. You're out of touch.
    *(to others)*
Let's go throw javelins.


*PISASTRATUS exits with others, leaving SOLON alone.*


SOLON
We could prosper in peace,
but all our culture's drilled to war.
We amuse ourselves with combat exercises.
Politics is a game with words.
I've the wit to be a player—but
I've set myself alone by babbling poems.
How can I speak to my people, Apollo?


*Blackout*

# Scene Two:  Oracle

*Immediate scene change, SOLON still onstage.*
*Lights up to show the early Temple of Delphi.*
*It is a small stone structure.*
*On the porch before the door stands ION, the TEMPLE KEEPER.*


ION
How dare you tempt the god to talk? He hears
so many prayers. He wants sacrifices.

SOLON
I left my wife and children alone.
I walked a long, broken path.
I climbed up and over rock ridges,
winding above a steep gorge
to reach the god here.

ION
You must be weary, to hear the god.
The cliffs are a wall encircling our few
believers. They show how far we can fall.

SOLON
I've gone hungry for days.
Why won't the oracle speak to me?

ION
Your little gifts leave the god hungry.
Bring goats for the temple's big dinner.
Bring silver to please shining eyes.

SOLON

I'll draw the god close with plain words.


ION

The god of reason knows the price of gold.


SOLON

I gave up so much to make the few
poems I can offer to the god.


ION

Beauty brings its blessings back to the maker.
Thank the god of song, Apollo, for your joy!


SOLON

I have another humble offering.
I composed a few lines here, honoring
the founding of Delphi for Apollo.
Could the god accept my gift?


ION

Can you live with a riddle as a guide?
The wisdom of the snake is coiled inside.


SOLON

Will the Python sway to my new tune?


ION

Does it praise Python?


SOLON

Not directly, but…

ION

Too bad. Python pulls poor believers down.
She'll squeeze from your lungs your last,
most touching songs of pain and pleading.
The god of mice might squeak with you.

SOLON

I'm not afraid of old snake stories.

ION

The Python is closer than you think.

SOLON

I want the word of the god of reason.

ION

You must hear it from Python.
She seems to twist slowly, but
pounces fast and devastates.

SOLON

May Python hear me praise:
"The Dolphin of Delphi"
From the sea, suddenly,
a dolphin leaps into a ship.
The ship carries Cretan sailors agog
with faith in magic. The startled sailors
see god in the gasping, wide-eyed,
quivering animal at their feet.
They let the wind take them far,
guided they feel by god in the dolphin.
They crash ashore and head uphill

to find the throne of the new god.
They climb into this strange valley,
ringed by horned mountains, the earth split,
water source seeping from the earth, steaming.
Here they gave the first human prayers
to Apollo in the dolphin—at Delphi.

*PYTHON enters.*
*She wears a garment of snake skins.*

PYTHON
The dolphin dies, a tasty sacrifice.

SOLON
Did the snake god die?
Or does the snake still rule at Delphi?

PYTHON
Mother of god detested the snake cult.
Apollo at birth jumped up to kill Python.
Each tooth of the serpent sprang up as His
army! I wear snakeskin in god's triumph.

SOLON
You wear slithery vestments
of the snake cult. You hide behind sleep
in their old home, then snatch their sacrifices.
You take the name of the snake god
—Python! These empty amazements
make riddles of sunlight and reason.
Using shed snakeskins as straps of leather,
you'd bind us to god with broken patterns.
How can you speak for the god of clear mind?

PYTHON
These traditions pacify teething armies.
They hear god in every fading echo.
Reason keeps peace with the dragon's teeth.

SOLON
Can there be peace?

ION
 Oracle has spoken.

SOLON
I have more questions, please!

ION
You get just one glance from this god.

SOLON
Can there be peace? In Athens, I hear
the dragon's teeth gnashing. I hear growling
inside the great silence about war.

PYTHON
A thousand years
have fled in tears
the Greeks burning Troy.
Men of iron will destroy
thousands more
cities and years before
the end of war.

ION
Oracle has spoken.

SOLON
That cannot be the voice of the god
of clear mind, hissing from a snakeskin,
promising blood and tears.

PYTHON
Solon of Athens, you trouble the god.
You risk your life in a thin ship, racing
faster than death to the priests of Egypt.
Then you whine about the walk here.
The mountains protect our sacred spring.
Egypt's barbarians pray to a cat-god,
dog-god, crocodile-god, hawk-god, god-kings.
But now you complain of our native rites.
Egypt made you mad.
You've too much faith in your own words,
because a few priests of Egypt applaud.
Ask them about reason and hear weird tales.
The god forbids you to go to Egypt!

SOLON
I had come to ask blessings
for another safe passage.

PYTHON
The god answers before you ask.
Go home. Take care for your city.
Do not go to Egypt.

ION
Oracle has spoken.

SOLON
I will not go to priests of Egypt,
but stay to worship you, Apollo!

PYTHON
Then you will embrace Python.

*SOLON goes to PYTHON.*
*THEY embrace.*

Take off this skin.

*ION removes the snakeskin.*
*PYTHON is a young woman in simple dress.*

I'm Themis, a woman of Delphi.
The Temple Keeper is my cousin Ion.
We have more to say about clear minds
for the days ahead. You'll share in the pure
ceremony of the true Oracle.
First I'll bathe in the spring of Castalia.
The snake cult robe is too hot.
You should eat from the temple offerings.

*PYTHON goes to a spring beside the temple, right, and rinses herself.*
*ION takes the snakeskin inside the temple.*
*HE returns with a bowl of food for Solon.*
*SOLON eats.*

PYTHON

It's too quiet in our temple.

Too few care for reason as a god.

At least, we need to build a road here.

A man of your devotion can be useful

to Apollo as the god's power grows.

Be sure. Apollo sees ahead

and his power grows. We of Delphi

know much about magic and mysteries.

We put them on and take them off.

Someday the god can stand sole and simple.

First Apollo of Delphi must rule

over all religious customs.


SOLON

Even the gods are ambitious in Greece.


ION

You would only worship a god with goals.


PYTHON

The women of Athens trouble the god.


SOLON

How? They are devout. They're reviving

the mysteries of the double goddess.


PYTHON

I feel no reverence for their get-together.

Their beliefs are ridiculous.

They did not ask Apollo's approval

to meddle again in old disputes

of sun and moon, new gods and old
goddesses, all men and women.

SOLON
No one knew Apollo demands this control.

PYTHON
Then no one knows their sacred duty.
Well, you knew it.

SOLON
And that is...

PYTHON
To come to Delphi, to hear the voice
of reason in religious matters, to ask
the Oracle and be guided.

SOLON
Tell them in Athens.

PYTHON
No! The god works from far away.
Delphi must not be thought to obstruct
the ancient worship at Eleusis.
The earth goddess seems strong now,
reviving from a long lazy slumber.
But the goddess of the mysteries is
very old. I'll tell you another secret,
from the one who sees ahead and strikes
all at once with arrows of iron:
the earth will endure us, but not as our mother.
The great goddess is about to die.

PYTHON *sits exhausted by the spring.*

ION
Tell no one of this prophecy.

SOLON
What could be more urgent to say?

ION
They won't believe you. Don't make yourself
an enemy of the women of your city.
don't expose Delphi to the last revenge
of the goddess followers as she dies.

SOLON
Is she ill?

*ION goes to PYTHON.*

ION
Themis, can I help you?

PYTHON
I won't do the snake dance again.
I'm clean of the snake. It's a goddess rite,
as old as the women's mysteries.
It's a lie to people of clear mind.
The source water rite is more pure.
That reveals the death of the death goddess.
She dies right here with the end of her dance.

*PYTHON goes into the temple.*

ION

Prepare yourself for the true Oracle.

SOLON

I'm afraid to face her. For her,
centuries bleed and the goddess dies.

ION

What will be your question?

SOLON

You've sworn me to silence about
the god's commands and prophecies.
How can I speak to my people for Apollo?

ION

Be one of our circle, an ally in Athens.
Build a road here. Protect our shrine, favor it.
Stand beside us and guard her right arm with
your shield. That's how to speak for Apollo.

SOLON

What can I say?

ION

Ask the Oracle.

*ION and SOLON go into the temple.*
*PYTHON lights a fire in a bowl on a tripod.*
*Then PYTHON sits on a tripod, stage rear.*

*On the tripod, her head is as high as a standing man's.*
*PYTHON wears a simple gown and a crown of bay leaves.*
*SHE holds a bowl and a bough of bay.*

ION
Laurel burns with barley and bay.
Here's Solon of Athens, who loves reason.

SOLON
War will prevail—but it's death
to say so in Athens. Our women rejoice
in the goddess—who's about to die.
What can I say to help my people?

PYTHON
Give blood to dead men, heroes in the ground.
They entered the earth to hold it for their sons.
Bodies in graves on Salamis face east.
They see nothing, until Apollo rises with
the sun piercing the earth to light their eyes.

SOLON
Salamis? Apollo points to Salamis?

PYTHON
Is that the way to your heart?

SOLON
I was born there and raised.
I fought for it. But we lost there, and
Won on the plain of Eleusis.
We settled the war where we were.

PYTHON

You hear a dragon's tooth army growling.
Throw it some flesh. Make it your beast.

SOLON

The punishment for war talk is death.

PYTHON

You have friends in Athens. Say just enough,
then steer straight down the middle. Blessed
is the city that listens to a single herald
—a leader inspired by Apollo.

*Blackout*

# Scene Three: A Debt Slave

*The scene is a crossroad of paths through farmland in Attica,*
*outside Athens.*
*SOLON enters.*
*On the other path, TWO ARMED MEN*
*enter with BOUND MAN TWO.*

SOLON
What is this?

ARMED MAN ONE
Process of law. Debt collection.

BOUND MAN TWO
A common sight!

ARMED MAN TWO
Step aside.

SOLON
Citizen! Your tribal leader approved this?

BOUND MAN TWO
Of course. I owe grain to his cousin.

SOLON
How much?

BOUND MAN TWO
Twelve bushels of wheat.

SOLON
Is that all?

ARMED MAN ONE
Debt unpaid, for seeds, tools, use of oxen
to plow, and a patch of land to till.

ARMED MAN TWO
And provisions to feed his family
until the harvest came in. A good deal.

BOUND MAN
Not such good land.

ARMED MAN ONE
Bad weather, whatever, the usual
excuses, laziness, fornication.

ARMED MAN TWO
We really must be going, citizen.

SOLON
What if I were to pay his debt?

ARMED MAN ONE
He is paying his debt - through servitude.

SOLON
Who can I see, to pay his debt and free him?

BOUND MAN
Deterios, of the hills tribe.
Please! Help my wife! She's pregnant!

ARMED MAN ONE
And then what? Who will trust his promises?
How will he find work? And the next debtor you meet?
You'll drive up the price of grain, once you start
paying for his kind, good sir. You'll go broke.

ARMED MAN TWO
Now excuse us, citizen. We have our job.

SOLON
We can't live like this!


*The ARMED MEN exit with BOUND MAN TWO.*


*Blackout*

# Scene Four: Home

*Scene: A courtyard in the home of Solon, Myrto and family, in Athens*
*SOLON and MYRTO enter together.*


SOLON
So, my messenger reached you.


MYRTO
Not long ago. I hurried.
It's a simple welcome.


SOLON
I'm so glad to be home.


MYRTO
Delphi, they say, is a difficult journey.


SOLON
Part of its allure. It's quite primitive,
for all its power. Will the boys join us?


MYRTO
They're at a friend's for dinner and the night.


SOLON
And the servants?


MYRTO
They fixed a light dinner,
and I dismissed them for the night.

SOLON
Fast work! Thank you. I'll be fast too,
to talk with you—about my love for you.

MYRTO
Over dinner first. You must want a good meal.

SOLON
You're my nourishment.

MYRTO
Eat slowly. Chew your food. Don't gulp.
And tell me. Did Apollo
bless your trade voyage to Egypt?

SOLON
No.

MYRTO
Oh.

SOLON
The Python said not to go.

MYRTO
Are you sure? What was the riddle?

SOLON
No riddle there. She said it directly.

MYRTO
How strange.

SOLON
She said I have duties in Athens.
She wants me to lead. The riddle: I have friends
here and must lead them straight down the middle.

MYRTO
Down the middle…

SOLON
Of divisions tearing the City apart, I think.
Between rich and poor, between tribes,
the hill folk and townsmen, oligarch factions,
old families, young rivals—
Find the middle—to lead all, peacefully.

MYRTO
That's a high calling. And dangerous.

SOLON
No worse than a sea voyage.

MYRTO
The Oracle warned you off that. I'm glad
you'll not take that dangerous journey.

SOLON
So am I. And here, I have strong allies
—you, with all your wisdom and charm,
and now Python, at Delphi. She is

a fabulous poet, bold, spellbinding.
She calls the oracular out of the air.
She tricks with puzzles and mystification,
but out of all that, she opens a way
to see forward, not in what she says
directly, but as a guide for you to find
on your own what you must do.

MYRTO
My destiny?

SOLON
Our future, together.
Our city's future, and us at its heart.

MYRTO
Be careful. She misleads.
Remember, Kylon believed what he heard
at Delphi and tried to seize power.
His journey from Delphi to deaths at the well
of the Furies took only a few weeks.

SOLON
Yes, but that was thirty years ago, and
surely a different priestess. This one's young.

MYRTO
Isn't the priestess the voice of the god?

SOLON
So everyone says, but we each must
decide for ourselves what the god means.

Kylon was only an athlete,
Olympic champion, people's hero, yes,
but no poet.

MYRTO
Oh, he lacked the powers of a poet!

SOLON
He could not follow the sense of her verse.
That's all I'm saying.
He heard what he wanted to hear.
The Oracle's subtlety exposed his greed,
to everyone's benefit.

MYRTO
Not his.  Or his family's.

SOLON
Let's consider too what Cleinias said.

MYRTO
The ship-owner?

SOLON
Recently, he said to me,
"You have restored your family's fortune."

MYRTO
That's true. You have much to be proud of, Dear.

SOLON

We have enough wealth, not to make me
an oligarch, but able at least to sit
among the high nobles by birthright
and wealth and take part in our politics.

MYRTO

You can compete among the oligarchs?

SOLON

I'm descended from Codrus, the last king
of Athens, and through him descended
they say from Poseidon, the great sea god.
You see how I plow the sea.
It's in my blood. So is leadership.

MYRTO

Your father gave away his wealth to the poor.

SOLON

And you married me anyway.

MYRTO

I saw a good thing.

SOLON

I need your insight now.
Yes, my father felt the growing suffering.
He was a good man, with a great reputation.
That will help me too. And business success
abroad has taught me many of the world's ways.
Now, with debt enslavement growing here,

I should not venture off in a leased ship.
If ships and goods are lost... I'll owe too much.
I should be done with overseas commerce.

MYRTO

That's welcome news! I like when you think
Aloud with me, not in thrall to Python's
word games.

SOLON

I can lead with words, she said.

MYRTO

How can you trust her riddles?
She hides her meaning in mean tricks.

SOLON

I trust my understanding. Otherwise,
I know nothing. And I would not try to
seize power like Kylon. His mind was not
as fast as his feet and fists. I'll move up,
one step at a time, proving my worth.

MYRTO

Your business would be close to home,
And that's a relief for me, a joy, yes!
But politics would be all-involving.
What of your other love?

SOLON

I have no other love but you - and the boys.

MYRTO
Your poetry.

SOLON
I'll have it, as I'll still have you.
I'll use it, to sway minds. It's got rhythm.
They'll dance. But Python taught me much.
My lyric poems, that I thought leap like
dolphins in exaltation of the god,
mean nothing to Apollo, lord of dolphins.
There's only one subject. Coins rule us now.
Foreign coins float the rich, drown the poor.
Our people struggle on the edge
of chaos and tyranny, slaves to coins.
That's my new subject, and I'll say it aloud.

MYRTO
The oligarchs and their lackeys will laugh.

SOLON
I'll move men with humor, make them laugh
and follow.

MYRTO
Follow you where?

SOLON
Salamis!
I was born there. I'm a proud Athenian,
born in a place that is no longer Athens.
We need the island back, to control
the bay as our harbor, to free our trade.

MYRTO

Who will be of your party? Cleinias?


SOLON

Maybe. I consider him a friend.
He's our tribesman. And Pisistratus.


MYRTO

Your cousin? Of course, but he's still a lad.


SOLON

An energetic one. He's popular
with the young crowd and tells me they fear
for their future.


MYRTO

I like the new future
that you've dreamed up for us from Delphi.


SOLON

You like it?


MYRTO

Love it.


SOLON

Will you join with me? Guide my ship?

MYRTO

Through smooth seas to harbor. Yes!

I'm glad your seafaring days are over.

You'll be home much more and safer.

The wiles of Python, Priestess of Apollo,

have brought you home to me, to stay.

Every day, we'll share the joy in that.

I'm a convert. We'll follow Apollo.


*Blackout*

# Scene Five: Procession

*Scene: The marketplace of Athens, a large open area near a crossroads.*

*The flat-topped rocky outcrop, on which the Parthenon will be built centuries later, looms a distance away, rear, with a fortification wall on it. Center rear is the Royal Stoa, meeting place of the lords of the city, with a porch.*

*The CHORUS OF WOMEN, including MYRTO and BASILINNA, enter from left and arrange into formation.*

*MEN gather to watch, including, separately, SOLON, PISASTRATUS and CLEINIAS.*

BASILINNA
Step up. In order. Now we do our song.
We chant till the lords of the city come out
of the long house and the Archon raises
his scepter to salute us and speak. We start!
Hail earth's goddess and child!
They suffered enough.
Their steady tears dissolve in mild
morning rain.
They seed the rough
ground with nourishing grain.

CHORUS
We'll call out with joy tonight.
Earth Goddess, Moon Goddess,
We return to your rite.

BASILINNA
The fields round your temple
gave two crops each year,
till raiding fires burned and land was seared.
We filled your temple
to celebrate twice each year,
till hacked and speared men disappeared,
and peaceful gatherings scattered in fear.

CHORUS
Now we'll fulfill our long-broken promise.
We'll dance with you tonight
with the moon, Earth Goddess!
We return to your rite.

*The ARCHON enters from the long house, in ceremonial costume.*

BASILINNA
On the first day, we bathed in the sea.

CHORUS
All that is holy arrived here by sea.

BASILINNA
The next day, we stayed indoors and fasted.

CHORUS
Silence is where the sacred has lasted.

BASILINNA
Today we'll dance our way to Eleusis.

CHORUS
And renew in the moon the women's mysteries.

*The ARCHON raises his scepter.*

ARCHON
We're glad to see so many happy women.
We hate to see you leave for even one night,
let alone three. But we know you'll come back
from the goddess sharing the beauty of peace.
Thank you, noblewomen, for organizing again
this old dance that shakes the earth. Renewal
of these ancient rites is our duty
to all Greek cities, to all peoples
who live on the edge of the great sea.
The Temple at Eleusis guards the Gate of Horns,
threshold to the underworld and all the dead.
Eleusis is the center of life on earth
—and we're the masters of Eleusis.

BASILINNA
Thank you, wise Archon, for peace at last!
Quiet in the countryside allows
this rebirth of the women's procession
out of the city to Eleusis, sacred
to women, shrine of the earth goddess.

ARCHON

We'll live in peace. Above Megara is
a huge statue shining out to sea,
a gilded image of armored Athena,
for whom our city is named,
our protector, with a glorious shield.
Both cities at peace adore Athena.


BASILINNA

The bronze shield of Athena guards the path
of tradition beside the playful sea.


ARCHON

These rites were neglected twelve years in war.
Reconstructing the old way was hard work.
You are all to be congratulated.
The priestess of the temple has assured me,
though, that she held secret services
each year with a few temple dwellers.
That must have appeased the goddess,
who had a hand in the advent of peace.
Please include a prayer of thanksgiving.


BASILINNA

We will give thanks. This rite sustains
one echo of an older faith.
In a golden age, women led the tribes.
Earth was worshipped as a warm and
patient provider. All the Olympian tales
of clashing titans recall turmoil as
conquerors swarmed here, as women fell,
as war cries overwhelmed our thin voices

and Zeus and his fierce brothers took hold.
The old religion was driven underground,
to dwell with the dead who knew it and obeyed.
All we have left is this—the Eleusinian Mysteries.

ARCHON
Athena is goddess enough to refute
the women's latest claims of neglect.

BASILINNA
Athena shields a city of men.

ARCHON
We are ruled by our wives.
Go, enjoy your great and ancient party.

BASILINNA
Yes, we're eager to dance.
We'll follow the Sacred Way,
past the kilns and workshops of clay,
the paint shops and homes of the potters,
out of the city at the Sacred Gate,
then west, winding beside the bay.

CHORUS
(in different speakers)
Not far from the city wall, we cross
the first river, still laughing.
Lunch will be ready at Agrai,
on the Ilissos River—roast pork.
Many pigs are sacrificed, the approach
will smell succulent.

BASILINNA
We will not bring wine.

CHORUS
The rites of the goddess are older than wine.

BASILINNA
We'll drink barley juice with mint,
in plain satisfaction of our thirst.

CHORUS
(in different speakers)
The way beyond is difficult.
We climb into hills of steep bare rock.
We trace a narrow pass in a barren place.
We who dance joyfully out the city gate
will be humbled by the climb.
We'll see no way out, nothing but stones
ahead as the foot-cutting path.
At last, the hills fall open and show
below a fertile plain beside the sea.
We walk down to the sea.
We follow the shore, toward horned
Mount Kerata. By nightfall, with torches,
we'll cross the saltwater Rhetoi River.
Just over the river is the mystery
at Eleusis, Gate of Horns, the abyss
opening into the underworld.

BASILINNA
Only the women of Athens who
washed in the sea on the first day

and fasted inside on the second
can come now to Eleusis.

CHORUS
Let no man follow!

BASILINNA
These rites are secrets of women.
Intruders abuse the goddess—and us.

ARCHON
A man who violates the mysteries is
killed, since he seeks secrets of the grave:
Justice, plain and simple. All are warned.

BASILINNA
We'll sing of the goddess now, concealed
in her veils under many names. Let's dance!

CHORUS
Da—the first cry, the baby's word for all.
Da—Demeter—mother of all.

ONE WOMAN dances.

BASILINNA
Chaos was first, a woman made mad, alone
in constantly changing dreaming.
Her world was a whirl.
Then Eurydome danced out of a dream.
She danced naked in empty space
and set the winds moving.

She spun life out of motion.
Her active arms and legs, her swirling hair
created life around her. Dancing faster,
she gave birth again and again
to sun, stars, moon and
Earth with her broad belly.

*MORE WOMEN dance as places and goddesses are named.*

More and more goddesses joined in the dance.
Their names: first Gaia.
Gaia, goddess of earth, is mother.
Ocean was mother.
Phoebe the sun was mother.
Night, Tethys, Rhea, all are mothers.
Urania is mother of worlds.
Hecate from death and dark moon is mother.
The blood-driven, angry Furies are mother,
Megaro, Alecto, Tisiphone.

*ALL THE CHORUS are dancing.*

BASILINNA
Demeter is earth as nurturing mother.
She coaxes food from the ground.

CHORUS
Demeter, Ceres, Core, Persephone!

BASILINNA
And the mystery names—the beautiful baby.

CHORUS
Brimus! Iakchos!
        His little head is wreathed with berries!
Brimus! Iakchos!


*BASILINNA and the CHORUS OF WOMEN exit, dancing.*


ARCHON
Let no man follow!
Renewing the women's festival of
fertility should please even the gods
who miss the whiff of fresh
blood smeared on a spear.
These rites give birth to a new life—peace
after generations of war. Repeat
with us now, with the lords of the city,
the blood oath that ends war. By treaty
with Megara, the lands of Eleusis
are ours, the island Salamis is theirs.
To put an end to our long struggle,
there is no more discussion.
Megarians too took the blood oath of
silence about war. There and here,
the penalty for war talk is death.
We're weary of war and plans for war
and angry shouting always war. Repeat:
The penalty for war talk is death!


MEN
The penalty for war talk is death!

ARCHON

I'll enforce our new law as fiercely
as all the laws of Draco are kept: with death!

*The ARCHON exits into the long house.*
*MEN start to disperse. Some chat in the square.*

SOLON

Death is that way, so I'll go this way.
Or is it,
Death is that way, we all must follow.

CLEINIAS

Are you feeling well?

SOLON

I'm well enough for a man without wisdom,
but too ill to hear sense when men talk.

CLEINIAS

I heard you weren't well.

SOLON

I feel strong enough to scold the gods
for their incessant love of worship.

CLEINIAS

You didn't follow up on our talk of
a trade journey to Egypt this summer.
We were going to have dinner.

SOLON

I'm sorry.

Instead, I traded insults with some

conceited god. I walked to Delphi

to seek blessings for the sea journey,

but argued with Apollo about

his claim to Reason ruling this world.


CLEINIAS

Then you're in shock, from challenging gods.

What did the Python tell you at Delphi?


SOLON

She gave me work that pays no money.


CLEINIAS

Bad omen.


SOLON

Still, it's something to do.


CLEINIAS

Does the work require ships—paid in advance?


SOLON points to the ground.


SOLON

No ships needed to get here.


CLEINIAS

Yes, you can handle that, I see.

SOLON
My work's a poem.

CLEINIAS
Bad business. About the ground?

SOLON
No, dirt's for Demeter.
The wet nurse who created verse, Iambe,
laughed at the fat mother goddess and
her sighing airs. I do too.
Dirty Demeter plays in the dark tonight.

CLEINIAS
Take a rest. You've seen too much sun.

SOLON
I chase the Sun all day. It leaves with
a grand farewell, then soon shines behind me.
The Sun and I are both getting nowhere.

CLEINIAS
Rest. You dared the gods to strike you senseless.
They did, you see. Apollo took your reason.

SOLON
I'm sure the gods need it more than I do.
I live with blood oaths and silence.

CLEINIAS exits.
PISASTRATUS approaches, and SOLON draws him aside.

SOLON
Pisastratus, listen.

PISASTRATUS
How are you?

SOLON
I need help.

PISASTRATUS
So I hear. How can I help?

SOLON
What are people saying?

PISASTRATUS
That you've gone to Delphi and come back,
Restless and confused.

SOLON
Mad? Insane?

PISASTRATUS
No one's said exactly that to me.

SOLON
I want you to say it around.

PISASTRATUS
Why?

SOLON

It may give me cover to speak out.
I wrote a poem—a crazy one, useless,
dangerous, a death-defying joy.
This one says what can't be said.
This one hates the humiliating censor,
and all the hidden oaths of silence,
discreet omissions, polite evasions.
It reveals the mind of our moment blooming –
what's going on, not what we're told
must be thought, but bad thoughts, really
wicked funny stuff about too many gods.
It's about politics and truth, about money.
It's about a lovely island we can see
from here. I'll need a few brave listeners.
They'll soon see I make too much sense.


*SOLON and PISASTRATUS exit together.*


*Blackout*

# Scene Six:  A Mad Poet

*Scene: The marketplace of Athens, the same as previously,*
*but the pageantry is gone, and the place is empty,*
*except perhaps for a few peddlers. Morning.*

*PISASTRATUS enters with FARMER ONE, FARMER TWO, CLEINIAS*
*and OTHER MEN.*

FARMER ONE
I won't clap for a madman. It mocks him
meanly. How has Solon gone mad?

PISASTRATUS
He's possessed by Apollo since the oracle.

FARMER ONE
That must hurt. No wonder he howls.

PISASTRATUS
Or so he thinks, or so he says.
He's a poet, so he means something else.

FARMER ONE
I'll clap for his dolphins, if they surface.

FARMER TWO
Again? I've seen them too often.

FARMER ONE
They turn wine into water, like all drinkers.

PISASTRATUS

This is a new poem, a funny one.


CLEINIAS

Gone mad and writing more poems?
I won't watch a good man play the fool.
It's sad what's happened to him.
Egypt and Osiris of the sand
shone too much sun into his head.
He rants against the gods.
They need to know he means something else.


FARMER TWO

If he speaks strangely, he says what's true.
The city is eerie.
Why did we let the women go? Are they safe?
What are they doing? Some say they kill piglets.
It's not right for mothers to use knives
to chop up little pink squealers.
It's an angry game of baby killing.
That's what they do, in a rage at men too.
They'll cut and murder a man who sees
their nasty spectacle.


FARMER ONE

That's crazy talk.
They celebrate vegetables—
fertility, seeds, sprouts, flowers.
Demeter is goddess of the ground's harvest.
She doesn't need the sacrifice of one pig.

CLEINIAS
They elect leaders and talk about politics.
They praise Demeter as the Lawgiver.

FARMER TWO
That's worse. It's really a rebellion.
When women carry shields like Athena,
then they can command the fighting.

FARMER ONE
But war talk is behind us.

CLEINIAS
Then what is politics?

FARMER TWO
I tell you, they took knives to kill little
pigs. They throw pig meat on the ground,
for fertility, all over the fields.

FARMER ONE
They should not be allowed knives.
Sacrifice is a men's ritual.
No wonder they keep it a mystery.

CLEINIAS
It's a strange city without women.

FARMER TWO
With women gathered, meeting outside the walls.

FARMER ONE
Here comes Solon, with a funny hat on.

PISASTRATUS
Watch this. He needs our support.

*SOLON rushes into the market. He wears a felt cap.*

FARMER TWO
Nice hat.

SOLON
It's Persian armor. It breaks arrows of straw.
It serves as well as anything to
protect a poet, who must stand alone
as a fool in the market, to speak to men.

FARMER ONE
It keeps the sun off your head. That may help.

SOLON
But the sun god's inside, burning my reason
to send a little light out my eyes.

FARMER TWO
How dare you speak of gods like an illness?

SOLON
I was taught to speak by a creature
who loves to command. He says, god, god, god
in a big voice all the time.

*SOLON steps onto a small platform, a messenger stand.*

FARMER ONE
Where are you going?

SOLON
Where have I been?
I'm a messenger! I heard words in
the wind from a land called Taboo,
calling forbidden things we have to do.
Can you hear the breeze rising off the sea?
Does it say, "Salamis," or just to me?
And whisper seductively?

FARMER TWO
Take off your clothes!
Let's see how great your madness grows.

SOLON
I'll tell secrets you know but won't say,
about a bare beauty right there in the bay.
It hides in silence, death's calm disguise,
but taboos can't close our eyes.
I'm alive and sing what I see.
An island in the bay appeals to me.
It sings, "Salamis! Salamis!" And what's more,
it promises great triumphs in war!

SEVERAL
No!

FARMER ONE
Let's help him down. He is mad.

PISASTRATUS
Please pity a good man driven by gods.

FARMER TWO
The gods despise him, to drive him so low.

SOLON
Words in the wind whisper Taboo,
Promise forbidden things we have to do...

FARMER TWO
Treason!

FARMER ONE
He doesn't know what he says.

FARMER TWO
The Archon should know about this.

*FARMER TWO goes into the Stoa.*

SOLON
Commanded silence hides the hell I've been.
My madness will end as your outcries begin.
I offer a song, not a speech, you know.
Apollo suggests the way it might flow.
I come from Salamis. I want to go back.
The swiftest way is called an attack.

SEVERAL
No! Get down!

FARMER ONE
Take care for your life.

*FARMER ONE reaches a hand to SOLON.*
*PISASTRATUS and CLEINIAS restrain FARMER ONE.*

PISASTRATUS
Humor him. It's a poem.

*The ARCHON comes out of the Stoa.*
*FARMER TWO follows and rejoins the crowd.*

ARCHON
What is this insult to the day's peace?

FARMER ONE
He's gone mad. We'll get him home.

SOLON
Insights of fire burn the hell I've been.
My madness will end when your good sense begins.

ARCHON
Solon, what message impels you to stand
like a herald before the long house of lords?

SOLON
All that cannot be said spills out of me,
half-accomplished, like our destiny.

ARCHON
The destiny of Athens is far off
indeed.

SOLON
It's as close as Salamis.

ARCHON
Now we can get there in peace and pleasure.

SOLON
Athens will never fall to the gods.
The gray eyes of Pallas Athena show
us favor in the long gaze of the gods.
But the foolish greed of our people can
lay waste our city. We can't help ourselves.
The riches that dress this latest parade
were stolen. Robbery is what I denounce.
Now so many with nothing owe all to the rich.
Tell me again, why must we pay those who
are already rich? What game is this?

ARCHON
Charges should be made in public assembly.
False charges will be punished.

SOLON
Justice looks on patiently. In time,
all will be punished for crimes of many.
Even the arrogant pleasures of the loudest
of the rich end early, scared by the numbers
of poor, landless, workless people, staggering

in the streets almost unseen, like ghosts of
citizens who could have been our strength.
Nowhere to go, their need is naked.
We all feel winds fleeing our cold faces.

PISASTRATUS
It's a real poem!

SOLON
Our laws make us slaves to other men's money.
Citizens of Athens enslaved for their debt!
Our brothers chained and grabbed from
their homes to be sold, to stoop and
sweat for strangers harshly, animals, slaves.
Our leaders do nothing. It's a matter of money.
Such wickedness will enter every home.
No one's door keeps out so determined
a thief of hopes. Alone in our homes,
we too are enslaved.
This bitter message my heart makes me bring.
When justice arrives, then wisdom can sing.

PISASTRATUS
Good! Good!

PISASTRATUS leads tentative applause.

ARCHON
So, you bring old news
about the unfortunate debt situation.

SOLON

I have better news.

ARCHON

That would win better applause.

SOLON

But worse news first. Conflict!

ARCHON

We knew conflict over debt as civil war
just one generation ago. The horror
ended in Draco's iron laws—that I enforce!

SOLON

Ours is the peace of quiet shame.
And we are in great danger.

ARCHON

You're the most in danger.

SOLON

The women are the most in danger. And now.

   *Silence.*
There will be a raid on the women.

SEVERAL

How? What?

ARCHON
How do you know?

SOLON
Words in the wind whisper Taboo,
calling forbidden things we have to do.

SEVERAL
Tell us!

SOLON
Condemned by jealous gods to dwell among
the forbidden, humiliated, silent,
I stared out to sea toward Salamis.
I saw the young men there leap into
swift ships, bold pirates and rebels
with contempt for peace-loving Athens.

ARCHON
You can't see that far. And to see
the intentions of men? Could they not
just be fishermen setting off?

SOLON
I knew it wasn't real, not yet.
But this strange dream made me mad –

ARCHON
Oh, a dream!

FARMER TWO
He is mad!

SOLON

—to press our just claim
to Salamis, land of our ancestors.

ARCHON

Tell us your better news and be gone.
If you talk nonsense again about war,
under the law, you will be put to death.
Do you hear me, madman? No war talk.

SOLON

The good news gives us land, to pay off
the rich and feed the poor, land for all.
The good news is a great common cause,
uniting the city in glory.

ARCHON

What is the good news?

SOLON

The good news is we can fight back the raid
on the women, save them, and win Salamis!

ARCHON

Seize him!

SEVERAL

No!

*A scuffle starts.*

ARCHON

The penalty is death!


SOLON

Gods, forefathers, sacrifice, duty,
honor, strength, power, right, united—
now it sounds like a speech from a lord.
But I had to face the forbidden. I saw
war coming, the war that's here,
but I'm forbidden to speak about it.
I'm sorry, it's made me crazy. Megarians—


*The scuffle stops as men listen.*


—took Salamis from our ancestors.
That same pirate spirit fills their swift ships.
Now they'll steal our good women.
War's already begun. We're late.


ARCHON

Now that this has been alleged,
we must check the safety of the women.


PISASTRATUS

Let Solon lead an armed group there!


FARMER ONE

Solon should protect the women!


ARCHON

Solon has been talking crazy
And illegally. Pretending madness?

So now we must put him in command?!

PISASTRATUS
He already leads us.

FARMER ONE
The law of silence drove him mad
with what he must say to warn us.

SOLON
Give me one night.
Let me act on this dream of danger.
Let's go in arms to defend our women.
If I don't find attackers, banish me.

ARCHON
If you've stirred so much mischief
as a war party on a bad dream,
you'll answer the law of silence
about war with a gasp at death.
We'll take up this matter again, when
the women are safe inside our walls.

SOLON
Thank you, wise Archon, for this chance.
I love the laws and answer with my life
for the women's safety and for peace.

ARCHON
Solon can lead a small party, to watch over
The women's gathering—but do not spy
On their secret rituals. Keep your distance.

Form your party and move fast as dreams.

SOLON
Pisastratus and I will go in a small boat to scout.
Revered Archon, please pick volunteers.
Get twenty assembled and ready in an hour.
Send them ahead with a good captain
to meet me at the Rhetoi River bridge,
at dusk. If I'm not there, they should press on,
to guard the women.

ARCHON
I'll follow with
a larger force and three days provisions.
We'll make a night march on the Sacred Way,
and escort the women home when they're done.

SOLON
Friends, please call your friends to arms!

ARCHON
The rest of the city can guard the walls.
This supposed raid may be a diversion.
Be careful of ambush, on your march.
And the ships at harbor must be guarded.

SOLON
Oh, and the first force, that meets me, must
bring women's robes and headdresses.

ARCHON
Women's clothes?

SOLON

Yes, women's clothes for each,
including headdresses. Let's go! Let's start!
Call out your friends to save the women.

ARCHON

Solon, I cannot ignore such a dire,
public claim of danger to the women.
But after all this fuss and panic, if
your claims are found untrue, a reckoning
will follow. You will answer
for your outrageous allegations and
violations of the peace, as the law
silencing war talk requires—with death!

ARCHON *leads the men off with shouting and cheers.*
SOLON *and* PISASTRATUS *remain.*

PISASTRATUS

You found your voice.
One strong voice can lead to new harmony.

SOLON

I'll resolve our civil unrest.
I'll cleanse the city of the blood
curse of Athens, from the civil war
and the killings at the shrine of the Furies.

PISASTRATUS

You'd have to be archon to do that.
You can talk the Archon out of power.
You'll say anything! You'll be a strong leader.

*SOLON steps down from the messenger stand.*

SOLON
No, the people will lead, the Archon enforce.

PISASTRATUS
And you'll lead the people.

SOLON
I'll dedicate myself to ending enslavement
of our poor for their debts.
That's the true curse upon our city.

PISASTRATUS
You touched us all with those lines.

SOLON
Nothing is more wicked than how we treat
our poor companions, with debts and fetters.
They need the ancestral lands of Salamis.

PISASTRATUS
So, you dreamed about a raid...
and if the raid doesn't happen, you die?

SOLON
Then we must make it happen, cousin.
I need your help—need it now, desperately.
But beyond is the prize. Work with me, and
you'll be a hero! A leader too!

PISASTRATUS

What do we do?

SOLON

Come with me in a small boat, round the Cape.
You'll set me ashore near Eleusis, then
dart to Salamis. Tell them our women
in the heat of fertility rites
want men, where our men are forbidden.
Say the Athenian girls to celebrate
want to share sweet peace with Megarians.
Say they are lustful under the moon.
I'm sure these promises will reveal
the evil in the men of Megara,
who would abuse us with our women.
Whatever you say, get a few to come,
get four or five of them to the beach near Eleusis
tonight, and drunk. They should run from their ship
to our women. We'll be waiting.

PISASTRATUS

What if I say, No?

SOLON

I  go alone—and die.

PISASTRATUS

I have no choice. You think up the damnedest
adventures and thrust them on me. Thank you,
I suppose. Will the women be safe?

SOLON
Yes, with us!
Pass this temptation among Megarians,
with plenty of wine, then get away.

PISASTRATUS
I don't know if they'll believe me.

SOLON
If they don't respond, my heart is a lie.
They'll come for our women, or I should die.

PISASTRATUS and SOLON exit.

Blackout

# Scene Seven:  The Rites

*Scene: dusk, at the grotto at Eleusis.*
*At rear is a cavern in a rocky hillside.*
*Front left is a stone well.*
*HIEROPHANT comes out of the cavern mouth.*
*She is the Priestess of the Double Goddess.*
*SHE wears a miter in the form of a pine cone.*
*TWO FEMALE ATTENDANTS flank her, with a basket and winnowing fan.*
*A WOMAN enters.*


HIEROPHANT
It gets late. We've waited twenty years
for this return. No longer. Are you ready?

WOMAN
Basilinna is coming.

*BASILINNA enters with OTHER WOMEN, including MYRTO.*

BASILINNA
Hierophant! Priestess of the Double Goddess!
We've been busy in our meeting.
We're nearly finished—or ready, yes, now.

HIEROPHANT
Do you speak for the women's assembly?

BASILINNA

I believe so, yes, though some have doubted.
  (*Calling offstage*)
Hierophant calls us to the mysteries!

HIEROPHANT

Where are your flowers?
Each initiate must carry a palm leaf
and a flower plucked by Persephone.

BASILINNA

We just broke from our meeting...

HIEROPHANT

Bring iris, crocus or tiny violets
gathered in blue profusion in the shade,
or hyacinth, narcissus, poppy.
Gather bouquets together, as girls have
always done.

BASILINNA

We're nearly ready.

MORE WOMEN *enter, carrying flowers or palm leaves.*
ONE OF THEM, EUTURPE, *gives Basilinna a flower and palm.*

HIEROPHANT

Tell me about your assembly.

BASILINNA

As guardians of faith's traditions,
We women hoped to celebrate
our ceremonial allegiance. But
my resolutions honoring home life
were hooted down, with cries of poverty
and stress embittering families.
Women shouted over debts and slavery.
Then came the claim of a blood curse
on Athens, guilt for hostages and murder
in the last generation's unrest.
Blame was all but named on great families,
who much resent memories cast as murder.
Some would re-enact our old civil war.
It was a lively meeting.


EUTURPE

If I may...


BASILINNA

Yes, speak, please, I hope in harmony now.


EUTURPE

I spoke out against the empty phrases
on our agenda. Basilinna and the noblewomen
were humbled by the rage of many women.
But she is our leader. She revived this rite,
once the Archon made peace and won
this sanctuary, where women can talk
and plan for the city. She leads Athens.
That's the true resolve of our assembly.
Peace lets us now resolve our disputes

in free discussion. We won't be stifled
by loud distracted shouting about war.
Basilinna has women's support
this year and forever in peace and silence
about war, to work out our true being.
That's the resolve of the women's assembly.

HIEROPHANT *looks out over the assembled women.*

HIEROPHANT
We begin!
These bold beauties show brief delights.
Persephone, girl of the goddess, reached out
to hold narcissus in her slim young hands.
Her friends laughed, and a light breeze
touched meadows with sweet scents to please her.
She was the future. But suddenly a fast
dark horse stamped the ground, echoing.
A great lord reached down and pulled her hair,
grabbed her arms and lifted her, struggling,
across his huge, sweating horse and rode off.
Wander the edge of the churning sea,
There's no answer to the mystery.
Only Hecate, stirrer of witches, heard
a startled cry from the girl pulled to hell.
So witches will always from gods rebel.
Demeter was frantic for her daughter
and searched the vast surface of the earth.
A weary woman, she wept at that well.
She knew then: her daughter had been taken
by the god given hell, Hades, old lord
of the dead. Hades desired her, took her.

Persephone, a child, was stranded
in eternal darkness, at the side of death.
Huge old Hades kept her close to pet her.
Call her condition "bride" as a courtesy.
Awful glory to be Queen of the Dead.
Her grieving mother wept at that well.

THE CHORUS *dance around the well.*

CHORUS
Circle the well, where women meet.
The common place where mothers mourn
is ground from which new life is born.
It shakes to the rhythm of our feet.

HIEROPHANT
Dance with the rising strength of joy.
The bride of death gave birth to a boy!

AN ATTENDANT *opens the winnowing fan to reveal a doll of an infant.*

CHORUS
  Brimus! Iakchos!
His little head is wreathed with berries!
  Brimus! Iakchos!

THE ATTENDANT *carries the baby, high in the fan, into the Chorus.*
THE CHORUS *dance around the baby.*

HIEROPHANT
She who stays in utter darkness,
Queen among the dead, gave birth

in life's triumph. Celebrate our harvest.

CHORUS
Brimus! Iakchos!

HIEROPHANT
Mystery: Who is Iakchos?
Fresh fruit of earth's enduring.
See the newest god, not of Olympus.
He subverts their thieving power.
Iakchos the baby god rattles old
thunder-mouth. His eyes need no lightning.
He seduces with a helpless smile.
Take this as your one dear lesson:
Persephone need never return.
We need no resurrections.
We dance on the ground though the gods don't sing.
We make music, while the mighty are silent.
Why nothing? Why silence?
The gods rule only the dead.
The secrets of hell expire in a baby's cry.
Sing the wisdom of Iakchos.

*HIEROPHANT brings forward the basket.*

These mysteries must be secret.
Mystic chant makes puzzles to hide the plain
truth that is magic from men who crave gods.
Initiates are sworn to silence.

CHORUS
We swear!

HIEROPHANT
Gods as destroyers must give way to love.
The Double Goddess nurtures in great harvests.
Let the virgins come forward –
well, all the unmarried—come forward
for initiation in sexual love.

*A YOUNG WOMAN comes forward.*

This mystery occurs, one with one, so often.

*SHE reaches into the basket as directed.*

Reach into the basket and take what you find
there, bend over for it, hold it—
yes, it's a phallus! A man's thing! Ha!
Thrust it in the cloth, enfold it and rub it.
That little gesture is the joke of love.
Release your hearts in laughter. Who's next?
Hurry? You all must do it. Quickly!
Lift your skirts to run for it.
Life needs no more than a few acts of love.

You'll make models of sex organs from dough
before dinner. Married women will show you
how to shape them with familiar fingers.

And you older women have your secret
rite with comb and mirror. Pull back your hair
and look in the mirror to see aging.
Does nothing come back from death?
Now—the last, most secret mystery:

there is life after death! Persephone
need not return—but she does return!

HIEROPHANT *holds up a sheaf of grain.*

Persephone was kidnapped by
Hades, Zeus and the god gang.
Demeter in anger blighted the crops.
Earth gave no bounty to hard labor.
Hungry people saw no honor in the gods.
The gods nearly fainted. Without our gift
of honor, the gods are nothing.
Desperate gods let Persephone go
free half the year, to keep the corn erect.
We wither like blooms, like weeds.
Our souls are wind-tossed seeds
of a hardy grain that sprouts again.
You as your love live forever.
That rebirth is the daughter of Demeter.

HIEROPHANT *raises the grain high.*
THE WOMEN *kneel.*
SOLON *enters with* A FEW SOLDIERS, *left.*
THEY *wear armor and carry shields and spears.*

SOLON
Please, excuse me.

THE WOMEN NEAREST HIM *move away at once.*
THE OTHERS *rise.*

Priestess of Eleusis...

HIEROPHANT
Sacrilege! Invading our mysteries!

SOLON
I'm sorry. I must...

HIEROPHANT
We'll have justice!

WOMEN *throw stones. A few brandish knives.*

MYRTO
Stop! It's my husband! Solon!
Why are you here?

SOLON
Danger! Pirates! Here! Attackers!
We're here to protect you.

HIEROPHANT
You've attacked us with spears!
We punish sacrilege with death.

SOLON AND SOLDIERS *move back under the assault with stones.*
WOMEN *with knives try to flank the small party of soldiers.*
SOLDIERS *hold them at bay by defensive gestures with spears.*
MYRTO *joins* SOLON *and they embrace.*

SOLON
All the men of Athens are behind us.
Pirates are coming to kidnap you.
They mock the mournful rites of Demeter.

They'd steal you like the girl goddess was.

BASILINNA
Pirates? Who would dare disturb the Goddess?

SOLON
Megarians! From Salamis!

BASILINNA
You lie!

SOLON
Then I should die.

BASILINNA
You shall die.

MYRTO
Hear him out! He's come to help!

BASILINNA
Only barbaric invaders attack shrines.
Megarians are neighbors and Greeks.
They would not attack the rites of their own
great earth goddess. They would not
come running to the Grotto of Hell.

SOLON
Pirates will take you off in chains.
Do as we ask, great Queen. The Archon
made me leader of your protectors.

BASILINNA
He can't. Tribal law forbids men to meet
while we celebrate the mysteries.
It prevents this sort of mad activity
undertaken in the absence of your wives.

SOLON
There was just a call to action in danger.
We must get ready to fight off raiders.

BASILINNA
Where's the rest of your war party?

SOLON
The first rank of fighters are nearby, and
forgive us, they're dressed as women
to draw the pirates closer and trap them.
Bring them here.

*A SOLDIER exits, left.*

BASILINNA
Your army dressed as women show delusion.

SOLON
We're here to protect you.

BASILINNA
All Athens knew you were ill lately.
You ranted against Apollo.

SOLON

Apollo angered me with his demands.

But He showed me danger, compelled me to act.


BASILINNA (to soldiers)

Why do you join this mad adventure?

For Solon's money? The Archon will reward

capture of the law-breaker. Help us.


SOLDIER

Solon saw the danger.


BASILINNA

He broke into the women's mysteries.

For that crime, he must die! And you too!


SOLDIER

This is for your protection.


HIEROPHANT

Share his delusions to your own doom.

These rites you disrupted were taught to Greece

by desperate refugees from war,

the suppliant maidens. To be given

shelter, each was forced into marriage.


CHORUS

On the wedding night, each killed her husband

with a hairpin thrust hard into his heart.


WOMEN *advance to attack the soldiers,*

*but the* SOLDIERS *keep them at bay with spears.*

HIEROPHANT
King Battus of Cyrene crept to spy
on women's worship.

CHORUS
He was cut open
at the altar like an animal sacrifice.

HIEROPHANT
King Pentheus of Thebes, dressed as
a woman like your fantastic handful,
joined the Bacchae in their dark night rites.

CHORUS
He was ripped apart by the wrath of
women. So was Orpheus, the poet.

SOLON
That's why we approach in armor and shields.

BASILINNA
And why we're forbidden to wear much.

CHORUS
Our skirts expose the fear of Athens.

BASILINNA
Long ago, the men took off on a raid, to seize
exotic, tall, carved olive wood images
of the old gods. Most of the men died, stranded
without food on an island and cut down
while starving. One man, one from all, returned.

CHORUS
*(in different voices)*
The women of Athens attacked him with pins
of their gowns, probing, thrusting, where is
my husband, father, brother, son? Women
in anger at war madness stabbed him to death.
So, now the women of Athens are forbidden
to wear large brooches or pins, dangerous
weapons! With little pins, we can only hold
together light skirts. But here, in our
mysteries, we carry knives and bloody them.

BASILINNA
You were fools to burst in here.

SOLON
I mean no disrespect, but I've no time
for your list of clothing grievances.
You'll soon see we're here to protect you.
See these brave youths dressed as women,
To lure Megarians away from you.

SOLDIERS DRESSED AS WOMEN *enter, left.*

HIEROPHANT
What sacrilege! You mock your women
in the shrine and presence of the Goddess.

SOLON
Good lads! Cute! Ladies ... They'll protect you.
You can help. You must be calm. Please stay here.
These youths will dance beside the sea.

We'll draw the pirates ashore and trap them.
Act as if you're still in the ritual.
Don't show fear, don't watch the beach.
Lads, let's see you dance. Don't laugh.
Your deeper voices will give you away.

*THE SOLDIERS DRESSED AS WOMEN dance, disorganized.*

You're each a frail and lonely beauty,
worshipping with wide arms, held high, the moon
that lights a stranger's way, hurrying to you.
Let him chase you up the slope toward us.
Hide your daggers till you reach the grass.

*THE SOLDIERS DRESSED AS WOMEN stop dancing.*

Near here is the grave of the happiest man
who ever lived, Tellus of Athens. He grew up
in a prosperous city as it grew,
and shared in its good fortune. He had sons
and saw his grandchildren romp in good health.
And he served as an old man in a battle
against the Megarian usurpers and
thieves who occupied Eleusis, here.
He strode into the worst fighting, to save men
wounded and down. His rush broke the enemy's
line, scattered them, made a rout. To do
so much, he took fierce wounds, gave up life.
Honor in his death perfected a good life.
He made Athens the masters here.
So dance with his happiness! Dance again!
Now dance on the shore! Go! Down to the sands,

where Theseus himself fought for Athens.

*THE SOLDIERS DRESSED AS WOMEN exit, right.*

Please go on, or pretend with your service.
We'll repay this dreadful intrusion
on your rites with honor for your courage now.
I promise, I'll build a wall to guard this
sacred site for women in the future.
Let's hide. Take off your helmet. It shines.

*SOLON and SOLDIERS go to stage, right,*
*where they crouch and watch offstage right.*

WOMAN
What do we do?

BASILINNA
Hierophant? Priestess?

HIEROPHANT
Many temples of the Goddess have been
sacked, looted, burnt. Invaders have taken
everything precious from the Goddess.
Priestess and vestal virgin have been raped
and enslaved. But the Goddess returns:
Peace made from fragments of old forms.
The Goddess reigns among the new gods.
Attacked again now, she will survive.
These are our mysteries. Someone will die
tonight. Let's pray for brave men of Athens,
who fight to protect us in our worship.

CHORUS
Goddess, protect them.

BASILINNA
The solemnities of war in rhythms
of death after death make doubt hide, silent.

HIEROPHANT
Our shrine is guarded by men of Athens.
Give thanks for our defenders.

CHORUS
Goddess, protect them.

*SOLON and SOLDIERS grow agitated.*

SOLDIER
A small boat has landed. Several men.

SOLON
We're just in time. Apollo told me their hearts.

SOLDIER
They're following the dancers, this way.

SOLON
Steady. Wait.

*SOLDIERS DRESSED AS WOMEN enter from right, dancing.*
*THEY cross the stage and exit.*

SOLON

Stand to arms! Guard the shrine!


HIEROPHANT

Who dares approach the Grotto of Hell?


*A MEGARIAN enters from right.*


MEGARIAN

What? Wait! What's this? I was invited!


SOLON

Lies!


*A SOLDIER kills the MEGARIAN with a spear thrust.*
*Shouting offstage.*
*SOLDIERS enter, with a wounded man on their arms, PISASTRATUS.*


SOLON

He's Athenian! It's Pisastratus!
He came with me.
I posted him lookout on the beach.


SOLDIER

We thought he was with the Megarians.


SOLON

You arrived just in time to save him!
He held an advanced, exposed position.


HIEROPHANT

Honor this warrior, wounded at the shrine.

*SOLDIERS bring in a SECOND MEGARIAN.*

SOLDIER
Here's a pirate.

PISASTRATUS
Kill him!

SECOND MEGARIAN
Sanctuary!
Mercy! We're at peace! You invited us!

PISASTRATUS
Lust lover! Lies! Silence the profaner!

*SOLDIERS kill the SECOND MEGARIAN.*

HIEROPHANT
Justice is done - as in all the old tales

*SOLON forms his SOLDIERS on guard again.*

SOLON
Hold your position. Stand guard.

*A SOLDIER enters.*

SOLDIER
There's maybe three dead Megarians down there.

SOLON
Did any get away?

SOLDIER
I don't know.
There's a lot of running in the dark.

SOLON
You men go to the water's edge, then
form a line, to scour the beach. Kill them!
No prisoners. As Hierophant says,
for their intrusion into the Mysteries,
the penalty is death. Search and make noise, signal.
Don't blunder and fight with friends in the dark.

PISASTRATUS
Let me lead them.

SOLON
Rest! Go, lads! Good work!

SOLDIERS exit, right.

HIEROPHANT
Solon, you saved us.

SOLON
Thank far-seeing Apollo.

HIEROPHANT
As Apollo approaches with his long bow,
even Zeus the almighty rises up off

his throne on Olympus, startled, worried.

SOLON
You won't know fear, within the walls I'll build here.

HIEROPHANT
Build walls, or our rites will never be restored.
In our first service in twenty years,
We've had to fight off pirates, had to break off
the ritual to kill intruders.
Blood is a bad offering to the Goddess.

WOMAN
Can we finish the service?

HIEROPHANT
No. Go home.
Get away from desecration. Flee it.

WOMAN
We can stay to guard the shrine.

SOLON
They attacked you, not the shrine. Kidnappers.
Slavers, rapists, pirates, blasphemers too.
You should get to safety, inside the walls
of the city. A large troop of our men
are fast marching here, armored for battle.
They'll stand guard over you tonight and
escort you home in daylight.

BASILINNA
Ladies, I brought you here and I'll lead you home.
We'll mourn this latest bloody sensation.

*A SOLDIER enters, right.*

SOLDIER
Two dead down there. And two here. None alive.

PISASTRATUS
I think that's all of them—all I saw.

SOLON
Take these bodies away from the shrine.

*SOLDIERS carry the bodies off, right.*
*PISASTRATUS exits with them.*

BASILINNA
Did our women's ritual die, too?

HIEROPHANT
No. This grisly outrage is its own new
mystery, but one we won't pursue.
We focus on the Double Goddess.
We must keep our worship warm in our hands.
It will flower again, like sustaining grain.

BASILINNA
Behind high walls?

HIEROPHANT
Yes! We'll be more secret -
and keep control of the invitations.


*HIEROPHANT, BASILLINNA and the WOMEN exit, left.*


SOLON
Go with them, Dear. Finish the prayers. I'm fine.


*MYRTO exits left.*
*SOLON is alone onstage.*

# Scene Eight:   The Goddess

*The Grotto of Hell at Eleusis. Night.*
*Continuous from previous scene.*
*SOLON is alone onstage.*


SOLON
Guilt—for luring men to die? Men who came
bounding at one word, to mate with our women?
Who scorned the men of Athens, because
we made peace? Who thought our wives would pant
under the moon in a mass for bold strangers?
A simple song of sex sent these men chasing
wild in the night to the Grotto of Hell.
Fools. More men move for steady drums of war.
I can set drums beating like hearts near
a new beloved, who smiles at fierce faces.
I pity these dead Megarians, sacrificed
to the god of reason, who makes words move men
but with poor little thought within the words.
How much more blood must I set spewing,
to lead Athens out of self-slavery?
To end enslavement for debt and unite
our city are great, honorable goals.
To liberate, I must first lead with blood.
But I feel no pleasure in it, except
as I too serve demanding, outraged gods.

*The goddess PERSEPHONE appears in the cavern.*

PERSEPHONE

You wish to be known as a leader of vision.
So have this vision—the Queen of the Dead.

SOLON

You're a local girl playing a part.
One of the Eumolpus family?
There's a sheep-tending poet who made
a good home and work for his children's children,
by reciting tales of Great Goddesses.
Get away with the others. You don't scare me.

PERSEPHONE

Would the Priestess abandon a girl here?

SOLON

She has many to care for.

PERSEPHONE

Believe as you please, your fate is set.
You broke off our ritual, and you'll suffer.
Your little trick triumph was just a start.
Your war will be bloody and indecisive.

SOLON

This week, we'll capture Salamis.

PERSEPHONE

Next year, you'll lose it again.
Have you forgotten in your games, that
Megarians too can fight and surprise?

SOLON
We'll win.

PERSEPHONE
You'll excite more wars.
It's all you know, to take the lead -
in the name of Apollo, nonsense of war.
What will you do, to give honor to Delphi?

SOLON
I'll build a road, so more Greeks can go there
to honor the new god.

PERSEPHONE
For the glory of Delphi in your next,
your Sacred War, you'll burn cities and
enslave the Greeks who live there.

SOLON
A Sacred War, for Delphi? Then I'll lead.
Your curses are childish, young lady.

PERSEPHONE
Does a girl know this: Solon dreams he will
end enslavement for debt in Athens.

SOLON
I gave voice in bitter verse about that,
from a platform to a crowd in the market.

PERSEPHONE

You'll free only men and only men of Athens.
Your wars will collar many Greek slave girls.
You'll build a brothel temple of
Aphrodite Pandemia, where slave girls
sit naked on linen, for free men to choose.
That's how you'll lead the men of Athens!
As a slave-trader! Pimp to the crowd!

SOLON

You're free with ideas.

PERSEPHONE

The Double Goddess, mother and daughter,
gives great bounties.
I'll inspire you to your ruin.

SOLON

I'm speaking up to stop slavery.

PERSEPHONE

Then free the women. But you won't.
They feed the freedom of your armed mob.
You'll lead your tribe by easing its unrest
for a while in action. You'll form
a close phalanx to crush other peoples.
You'll bask in idle glory in your loot,
but you won't give more freedom to Greece.
You lost your freedom when you made war.
That is the curse of the Goddess
on the mad poet of Apollo.

SOLON
The Goddess is mad, to punish Greece
for my follies. Strike me down.

PERSEPHONE
I was given to eternity in Hell,
mated to the old, dark god of the dead,
grasping, leering Hades. Why? Because
I split open one red pomegranate
and nibbled the fruit off a few little seeds.
There's not much pulp there, though it's tasty.
That act of hunger, with forbidden fruit,
banished me from lands of the living,
condemned a young goddess to dwell with the dead.

SOLON
Condemn me and not my people.

PERSEPHONE
Your poems will vanish. You've no time now
to nurture their growth. You're in politics.
Atlantis will stay beneath the sea.
Its moral lessons are drowned, lost,
because you fail now to save the story,
You'll leave your name—not as epic poet,
or lyric, not even comic. You won't
be remembered as a liberator!
Your name will be a mocking word—Solon,
a pompous incumbent, thinking wisdom's
spewing lots of solemn fussing about
Godlike traditions with an impulse to war.

SOLON

You're a clever girl and hurt me.

*SOLON starts to flee, left.*

PERSEPHONE

Do you still deny the desecrated
Goddess within me?

SOLON

No. Your invective's
too vast to be human. It must come from
Gods we can only adore for the ardor
of their long revenge on our ignorance.

PERSEPHONE

Our disgust is with your nasty prayers.
The pettiness and evils that people ask for!

SOLON

Those were not my father's prayers,
Nor my mother's, nor my wife's. And I -
I fought off intruders into your mystery.

PERSEPHONE

You drew trouble here with enticing lies.

SOLON

They showed their true hearts, as I could foresee.
I did, I will, protect your mysteries.

PERSEPHONE
Bring men to new rituals of our faith
at Eleusis. Men could do more for
Demeter, who is your mother too.
They could share in a mixed ceremony.

SOLON
Let me serve the earth mother.

PERSEPHONE
Double Goddess goes forward in the daughter.

SOLON
I'll serve you.

PERSEPHONE
Poor poet, your words will always be
confused by echoes of religious haunting.
You embrace the dead in shaded darkness.
This is my final curse: may you always
find words too meaningful, and weave shadows
of old faith in habits with no meaning.

SOLON
So, I'm condemned to eternal redemption.

PERSEPHONE
You're saved to seek it in animal whimpers.

SOLON
It's a deal then. I will serve you.

PERSEPHONE
Go squander your soul in busyness and scheming.

SOLON
That's just a good life, wasteful as the gods.

PERSEPHONE
The goddess now leaves the earth to men like you.

SOLON
I must leave the Goddess, to go plan
an attack on Salamis, to win land -
my birthland—to feed our city and
lead us out of slaveholding slavery.

*SOLON exits, left.*

PERSEPHONE
Abandoned among the dead, I see
the end of all their sanctimony.
In just a thousand years,
Zeus and Apollo die beside the mother.
I see horsemen invading, unopposed,
galloping through passes into Greece
as if they were racing in great herds.
Behind them follow men in thick hoods,
hiding their faces, chanting,
men who don't marry, who condemn our flesh.
They carry the child god Iakchos,
taken from his mother.
The baby shivers in their scratchy arms.
The world is as naked and new

after a thousand years.
They say nothing of the goddess,
but I will wait for them ahead,
among the dead.

WILLIAM CONSIDINE writes poems and plays. His previous books of plays include *The Furies* (The Operating System, 2017) and *Moral Support* (Finishing Line Press, 2025). His books of poetry include *Strange Coherence* (The Operating System 2013), *The Other Myrtle* (Finishing Line Press 2021) and *Continent of Fire* (Kelsay Books 2022). He was a member of the Playwrights Workshop of the New York Public Theater, and is a member of the Dramatists Guild, the Polaris North theater artists cooperative, San Miguel Playwrights, and the Brevitas poets' cooperative. He is an honors graduate of Stanford University and Harvard Law School. He has been a lecturer in law, an administrative law judge, an arbitrator, General Counsel for a New York City government agency, and Division Vice President for a public service organization in dispute resolution. See more about his poetry and plays at williamconsidine.com.